PAWSOME PUPPETS!

Make Your Own
PAW Patrol Puppets

T0016036

Pawsome Puppets! Make Your Own PAW Patrol Puppets
ISBN 978-1-948206-44-0

©2022 Spin Master PAW Productions Inc. All Rights Reserved. PAW Patrol and all related
titles, logos and characters are trademarks of Spin Master Ltd. Nickelodeon and all related
titles and logos are trademarks of Viacom International Inc.

All rights reserved. Published by Curiosity Ink Media, LLC. No part of this publication may be
reproduced, distributed, or transmitted in any form or by any means, including photocopying,
recording, or other electronic or mechanical methods, without the prior written permission of
the publisher, except in the case of brief quotations embodied in critical reviews and certain
other noncommercial uses permitted by copyright law.

Curiosity Books is a registered trademark of Curiosity Ink Media, LLC
www.curiosityinkmedia.com
Printed in China

PAWSOME PUPPETS!

Make Your Own PAW Patrol Puppets

CURIOSITY BOOKS

NO JOB TOO BIG, NO PUPPET TOO SMALL!

Calling all crafty kids! Are you ruff ruff ready for an artistic adventure? The PAW Patrol is here to help you create one-of-a-kind puppets! Just follow the step-by-step instructions in this book to make your very own handheld heroes. Once you've finished creating, this book will guide you in putting on your very own puppet show. The PAW Patrol is on a roll!

CAREFUL CRAFTING WHEN MAKING AND CREATING. IT'S IMPORTANT TO ALWAYS TAKE CARE!

- Always have an adult helper present when doing crafts, especially when using scissors.

- Cover surfaces and open the window when using glue and paint.

- Get permission to use any materials.

TABLE OF CONTENTS

PAPER LUNCH BAG PUPPETS

Start with a bag . . . but end up with a pup! With a little work and a lot of imagination, you can transform a simple brown paper bag into your very own playful piece of art. Follow the steps to create paper bag pups that look just like the PAW Patrol heroes!

WHAT YOU NEED

- paper bags
- paint
- paintbrush
- colored cardstock
- black marker
- safety scissors
- glue

WHAT TO DO

1 Paint the paper bag the color of your favorite pup's uniform. Let dry.

2 Position the bag so the opening is at the bottom and the base is at the top, folded flat and facing out toward you.

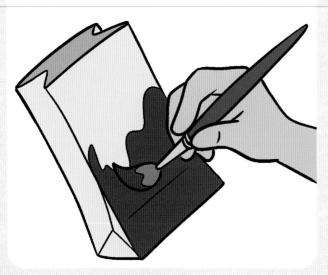

3 Push out the bottom part of the pup's face from the inside front cover. Add any details with black marker. Glue the face onto the bag. Let dry.

4 Cut out the pup's tail from colored cardstock and glue it onto the back of the bag, so it sticks out at one side. Let dry.

5 Pop out the pup's badge from the front of the book and glue it onto the body. Let dry.

ONE TEAM, ONE DREAM!

SOCK PUPPETS

Socks don't just keep feet—and paws—warm. They can be transformed into amazing creations!

Follow the directions to make your very own Chase puppet from a simple sock. This hardworking police pup is here to help!

WHAT YOU NEED

- tan or brown sock
- red craft felt
- brown craft felt
- glue
- safety scissors

WHAT TO DO

1 Cut an oval of red felt that is almost the same length of the sock from heel to toe. Cut another piece of red felt for Chase's tongue.

2 Spread the sock out, bottom and heel facing up. Glue the red felt oval and the tongue onto the sock.

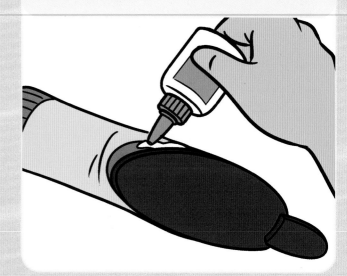

3 Cut two pieces of brown felt in the shape of ears. Pop out Chase's eyes and nose from the back of this book. Then pop out his badge from the front of the book.

4 Flip the sock over so the mouth side is down. Glue eyes, ears, and nose to the sock. Let dry.

5 Cut out the police cap from the back cover flap. Glue the ends together. Let dry.

6 Put your hand in the sock. Set the police hat on top of Chase's head and glue his badge to his front.

CHASE IS ON THE CASE!

POP-UP PUPPETS

Ice or snow, Everest is ready to go! These simple steps show you how to make a pop-up puppet of this lovable husky.

It's snow time!

WHAT YOU NEED

- paper cup
- paper straw
- colored cardstock
- black marker
- glue
- colored markers
- pencil
- safety scissors

WHAT TO DO

1 Cut out the front and back of the pup's face from colored cardstock. Add any details with black marker.

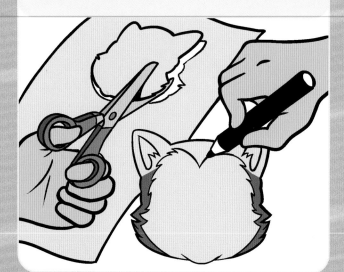

2 Pop out the pup's eyes and nose from the back of the book and glue them onto the front of the face. Let dry.

Glue the top of the straw between the front and back of the pup's face. Let dry.

Cut out the front and back of the pup's hat and glue it on top of the head. Let dry.

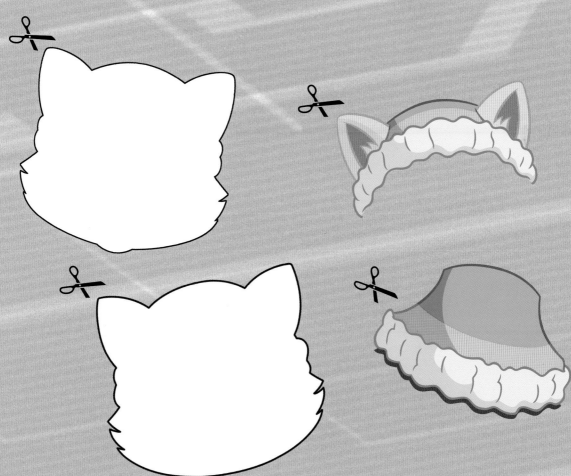

5 Use colored cardstock and colored markers to decorate your cup.

6 Push a pencil through the bottom of the cup and wiggle it around until the hole is big enough to fit your straw.

OFF THE TRAIL, EVEREST WON'T FAIL!

7 Stick the straw inside the cup and push it out of the hole at the bottom, so the pup's head is hidden in the cup until the straw is pushed up.

MARIONETTES

Ready for a jungle adventure? With this easy-to-make marionette of Tracker the jungle rescue pup, you'll be racing to the rescue in no time.

Just pull the strings and watch Tracker leap into action!

WHAT YOU NEED

- colored cardstock
- string
- safety scissors
- pencil
- card tube
- glue
- black marker
- paint
- paintbrush
- two craft sticks

WHAT TO DO

1

Paint the card tube the color of the pup's uniform. Let dry.

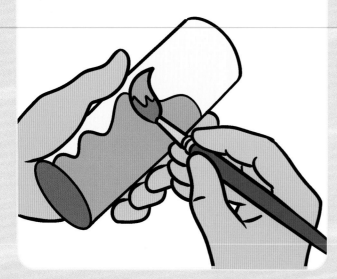

2

Cut out the pup's head, tail, and four paws from colored cardstock. Add any details with black marker.

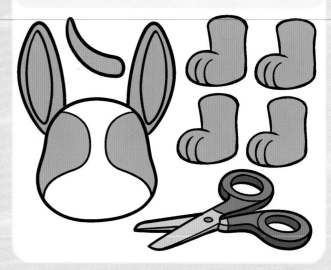

3

Cut out the pup's hat below and glue it on top of the head. Let dry.

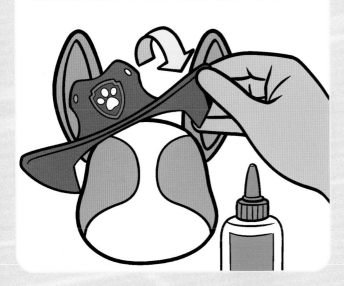

4

Push a pencil through the top of the hat and the bottom of the head, the top and bottom of the tail, the top and bottom of the front paws, and the top of the back paws.

5

Push a pencil through the card tube, once at each end on what will be the topside, and four times, once at each corner, on what will be the underside.

6

Cut two short pieces of string. Use them to attach the bottom of the head to one end of the topside of the card tube, and the bottom of the tail to the other end.

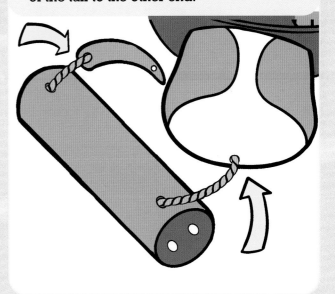

7

Cut four short pieces of string. Use them to attach the top of the paws to each corner of the underside of the card tube.

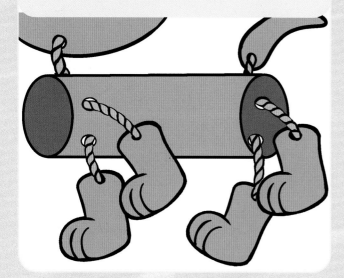

8

Glue the center of the craft sticks into a cross shape. Let dry.

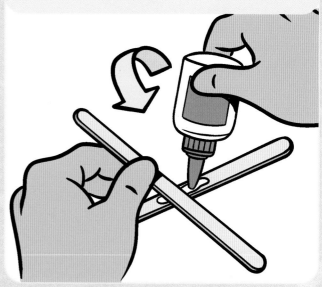

9

Cut four long pieces of string. Use them to attach the top of the hat, tail, and front paws to each end of the craft stick cross.

10

Pop out the pup's eyes and nose from the back of the book and glue them onto the front of the face. Let dry.

WELCOME TO

THE WILD SIDE!

FEARLESS FINGER PUPPETS

Want to make an easy craft that packs plenty of action?
Then, dude, it's totally time to dive into a finger puppet making adventure with Zuma!
This simple toy is the perfect way to capture the spirit of imaginative play.

WHAT YOU NEED

- colored cardstock
- safety scissors
- black marker
- colored marker
- glue
- brown ball of wool

WHAT TO DO

1

Cut out the pup's body and head from colored cardstock. Add any details with black marker.

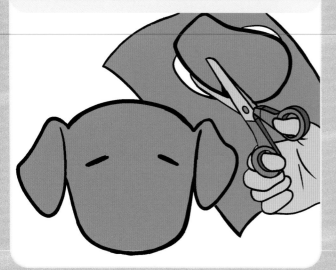

2

Cut out the pup's uniform from colored cardstock and glue it onto the body. Add any details with a colored marker. Let dry.

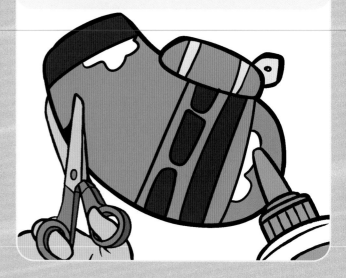

3

Pop out the pup's eyes and nose from the back of the book. Then pop out the badge from the front of the book. Let dry.

4

Cut out the pup's hat from colored cardstock and glue it on top of the head. Add any details with a colored marker. Let dry.

5

Cut lots of little pieces of wool and glue them on to make a tail. Let dry.

6

Cut out four holes, big enough to fit your fingers through, along the bottom of the body.

THIS PUP NEVER GIVES UP!

FUN FOAM FACES

Foam is a fun, flexible material used in crafting . . . and who knows more about building materials than Rubble the construction pup? This PAWsome activity is perfect for little heroes everywhere.

Pup, pup hooray!

WHAT YOU NEED

- colored foam pieces
- safety scissors
- craft stick
- glue
- paint
- paintbrush
- black marker

WHAT TO DO

1 Cut out the pup's head shape from colored foam. Remember to cut the shape twice, for the front and back.

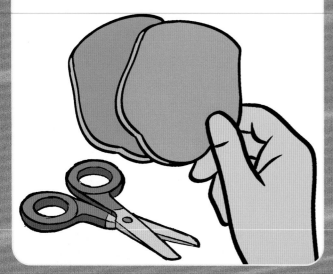

2 Glue the front and back head shapes together, with a piece of foam in the center. Let dry.

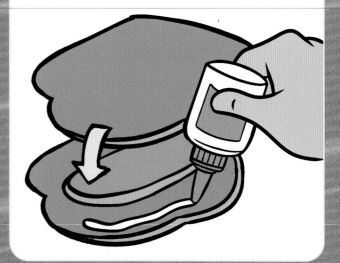

3

Cut out the pup's snout, ears, and eyes from colored foam.

4

Glue the face pieces onto the front of the head—layering them up makes the puppet 3D! Let dry. Add any details with black marker.

5

Cut out the pup's hat shape from colored foam. Remember to cut the shape twice, for the front and back.

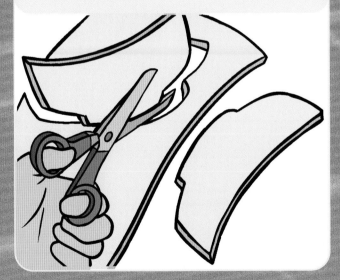

6

Glue the front hat piece onto the front of the head. Let dry.

7 Glue the back hat piece onto the back of the head. Then glue the craft stick to the back of the head, and paint it the color of the pup's uniform. Let dry.

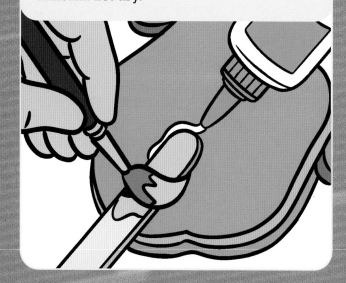

8 Cut out the pup's badge shape from colored foam.

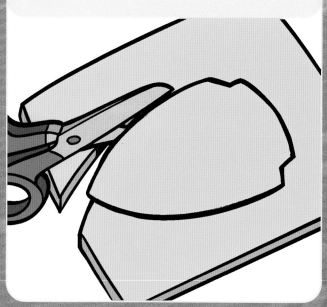

9 Glue the badge piece onto the front of the stick. Let dry.

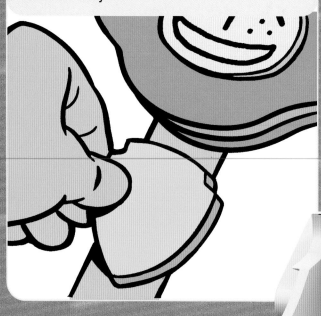

BORN BRAVE!

CRAFT STICK PUPPETS

Pup, pup, and away—it's time for a day full of play! Use your super maker skills to create a craft stick puppet of Skye, the high-flying cockapoo. Onward and pupward!

WHAT YOU NEED

- two craft sticks
- paint
- paintbrush
- black marker
- colored cardstock
- safety scissors
- glue

WHAT TO DO

1 Paint one of the craft sticks the color of the pup's uniform. Let dry.

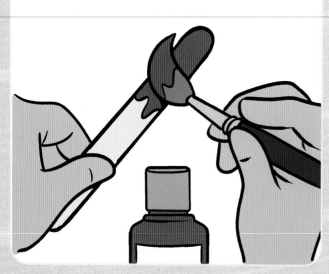

2 Cut out the pup's head from colored cardstock. Add any details with black marker.

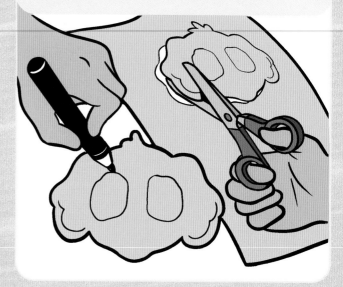

3 Pop out the pup's eyes and nose from the back of the book and glue them onto the front of the face. Let dry.

4 Pop out the pup's hat from the back of the book and glue it on top of the head. Then pop out the pup's badge from the front of the book and glue it onto the front of the craft stick. Let dry.

5 Paint the other craft stick the same color as the pup's wings. Let dry. Then, glue the second craft stick across the back of the first craft stick. Let dry.

SUPERSONIC!

ORIGAMI PUPPETS

Rocky loves to turn trash into treasures. Now you can transform paper into a puppet with just a few folds! Follow the instructions below to make your very own origami Rocky.

WHAT YOU NEED

- colored cardstock
- safety scissors
- black marker
- glue

WHAT TO DO

1
Cut the colored cardstock into a square. Fold one corner of the square over to meet the opposite corner, making a triangle. Turn the triangle so the point is at the bottom and the long, flat side is at the top.

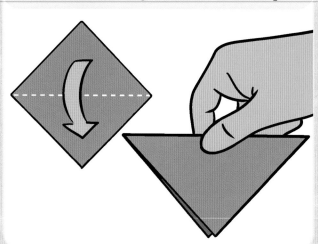

2
Fold down the top two corners of the triangle, to form the pup's ears.

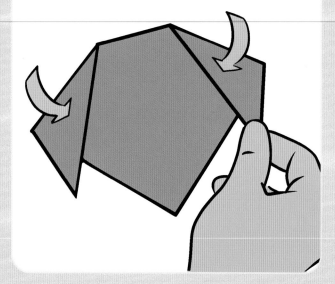

3 Fold up the top layer of the point, to form the pup's nose. Add any details with black marker.

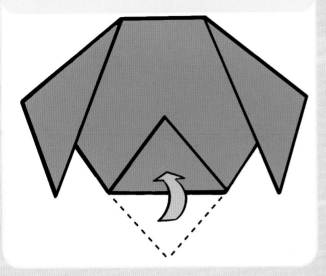

4 Pop out the pup's eyes and snout from the back of the book and glue them onto the front of the face. Let dry.

5 Cut out the pup's hat from the front of the book and glue it on top of the head. Let dry.

GREEN MEANS GO!

GLOVE PUPPETS

Ryder heads up Adventure Bay's bravest—the PAW Patrol! He always knows which pup is right for the job . . . and they are always here to help. Use your super skills to make a glove puppet of Ryder and Chase. It's teamwork time!

WHAT YOU NEED

- pair of gloves
- colored cardstock
- safety scissors
- Velcro® stickers
- glue
- black marker
- turn the page for prop ideas

WHAT TO DO

1 Glue one Velcro® sticker onto each finger of the gloves. Let dry. Keep the other side of each Velcro® sticker safe.

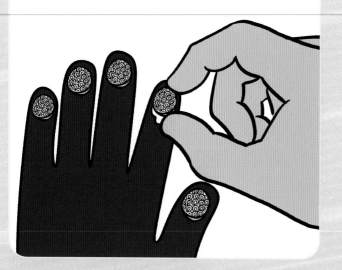

2 Cut out the pup's head and Ryder's head from colored cardstock. Add any details with black marker.

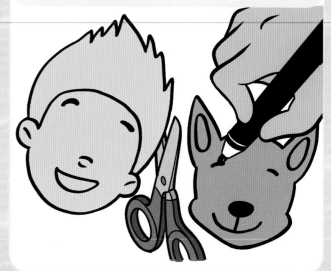

3 Pop out both of their eyes from the back of the book and glue them onto the front of the faces. Let dry.

4 Cut out both of their hats and glue them on top of their heads. Let dry.

5 Cut out four props from colored cardstock for the pup, and four for Ryder.

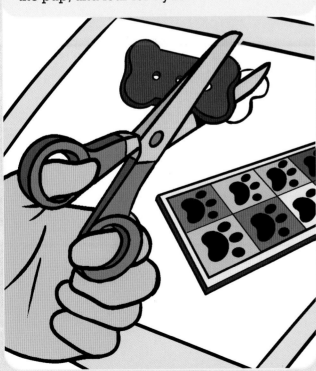

6 Glue the other side of one Velcro® sticker onto each prop. Let dry.

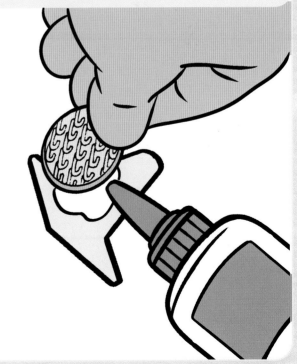

PUP PROP SUGGESTIONS

Whistle

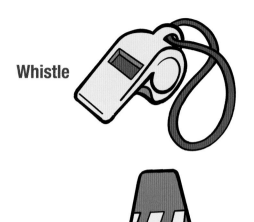

Flashlight

Traffic Cone

Net

Pup mat

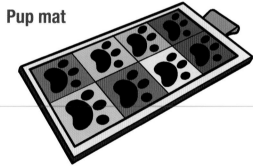

Binoculars

Bone-shaped pup biscuit

Pup gadget

PAW PATROL,
TO THE LOOKOUT!

FELT FINGER PUPPETS

Felt is super soft fabric, perfect for interactive play!
Use felt to make a finger puppet of Rubble.

WHAT YOU NEED

- colored felt
- safety scissors
- glue
- black marker

WHAT TO DO

1

Follow the template in this illustration to cut out the pup's shape from colored felt. Remember to cut the shape twice, for the front and back.

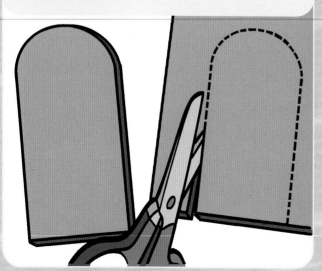

2

Glue around the outside edge of one piece of felt—leaving room for your finger in the center—and press the other piece of felt against it to make your finger puppet. Let dry.

3

Cut out two pieces of felt the color of the pup's uniform.

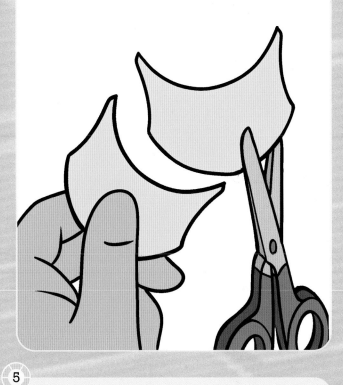

4

Glue one piece of the uniform onto the front, and one onto the back of the puppet. Let dry.

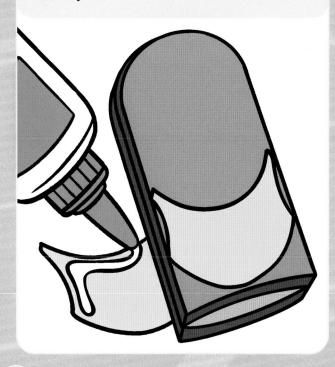

5

Cut out two pieces of colored felt for the pup's ears.

6

Glue the ears onto the front of the puppet. Let dry.

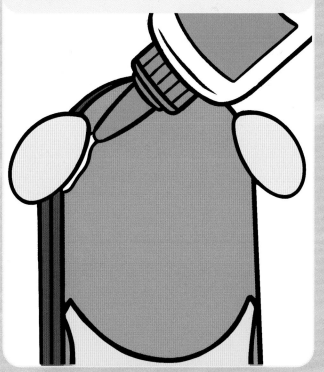

Cut out two pieces of felt the color of the pup's hat.

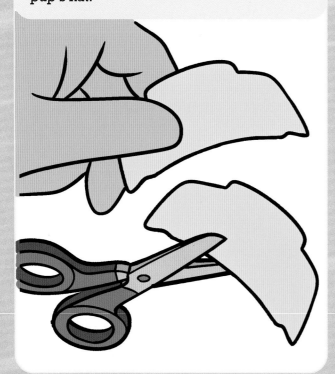

Glue one piece of the hat onto the front, and one onto the back of the puppet. Let dry.

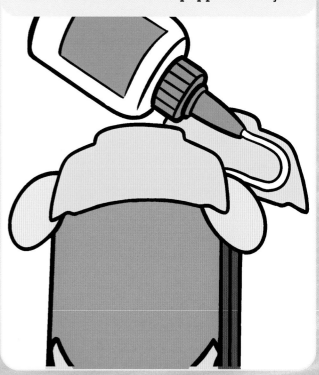

PUP POWER!

Pop out the pup's eyes and nose from the back of the book, and the badge from the front of the book. Then glue them onto the front of the puppet. Let dry. Add any details with black marker.

PIPE CLEANER PUPPETS

Pipe cleaners are safe and simple crafting tools, perfect for small hands and growing minds. With just a few creative twists, you can make the whole PAW Patrol team!

WHAT YOU NEED

- colorful pipe cleaners
- colorful small pom-poms
- safety scissors
- glue

WHAT TO DO

1

Pick a pipe cleaner the color of the pup's uniform and twist it lightly around your finger to create a spring.

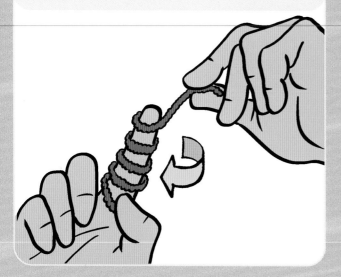

2

Pick a pom-pom, and glue it on top of the pipe cleaner. Let dry.

3 Pop out the pup's eyes from the back of the book, and glue them onto the pom-pom. Let dry.

4 Pop out the pup's badge from the front of the book, and glue it onto the front of the pipe cleaner spring. Let dry.

WHEN THINGS GET TOUGH, WE GET RUFF!

JUMPING JACK PUPPET

Skye is always excited for the next mission! This hardworking pilot pup jumps at the chance to save anyone in need. Use your new puppet to show off Skye jumping into action and jumping for joy!

WHAT YOU NEED

- colored cardstock
- safety scissors
- pencil
- four brads
- black marker
- glue

WHAT TO DO

1 Follow the template in this illustration to cut out the pup's head and body shape, and four leg shapes from colored cardstock.

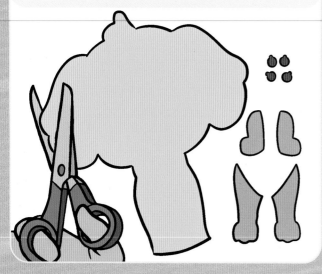

2 Pop out the pup's eyes and nose from the back of the book and glue them onto the pup's head. Let dry. Add any details with black marker.

3

Pop out the pup's badge from the front of the book, and glue it onto the front of the pup's body. Let dry.

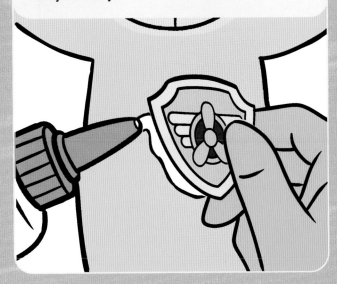

4

Push a pencil through the top of each leg shape, and four times through the body shape.

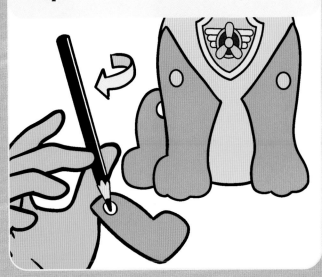

5

Attach the legs to the body using brads.

YOU GO, PUP!

TOILET TISSUE ROLL PUPPETS

Having your own Tracker puppet is easy when you follow these instructions! With just a few materials and little bit of handiwork, you'll be off on your very own jungle adventure in no time. ¡Al rescate!

WHAT YOU NEED

- card tube
- glue
- paint
- paintbrush
- colored cardstock
- safety scissors
- black marker

WHAT TO DO

1

Paint the card tube the color of the pup. Let dry.

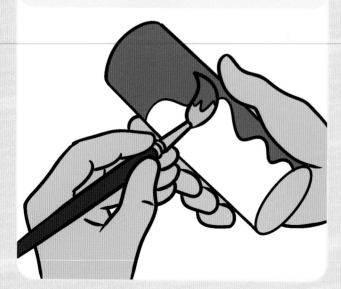

2

Cut a strip of cardstock the color of the pup's uniform and collar. Glue them both around the tube. Let dry.

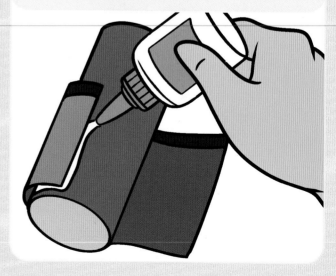

3

Cut out two large ears from cardstock. Glue them sticking up from the top of the tube. Let dry.

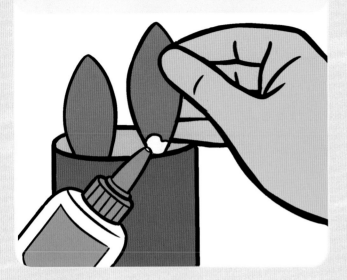

4

Pop out the pup's eyes and nose from the back of the book, and the badge from the front, and glue them onto the tube. Let dry. Add any details with black marker.

5

Pop out the pup's hat from the back of the book and glue it around the top of the tube. Let dry.

READY TO GO WILD!

SPOON PUPPETS

Rocky the recycle pup knows how to reuse everything. In this craft, you will discover a surprising new use for an item, just like Rocky! By taking an everyday wooden spoon and applying a few decorations, you can have a PAW Patrol play pal of your very own!

WHAT YOU NEED

- wooden spoon
- paint
- paintbrush
- ball of wool
- colored cardstock
- safety scissors
- glue
- tape
- black marker
- buttons

WHAT TO DO

1

Paint the base color of the pup on the wooden spoon. Let dry.

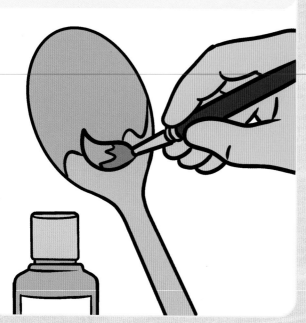

2

Wrap some tape around the handle so you can get a nice straight edge to paint the pup's uniform. Let dry, then remove the tape.

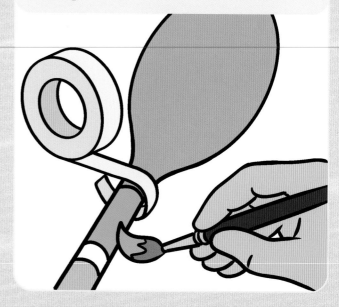

3

Cut out the pup's ears from colored cardstock, and glue them onto the top of the wooden spoon. Let dry.

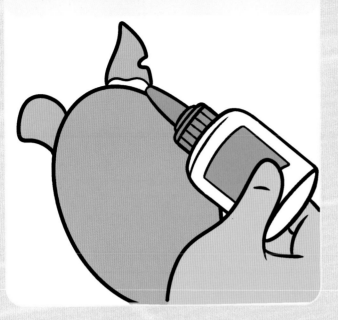

4

Cut pieces of wool for the pup's fur, and glue it onto the back of the wooden spoon. Let dry.

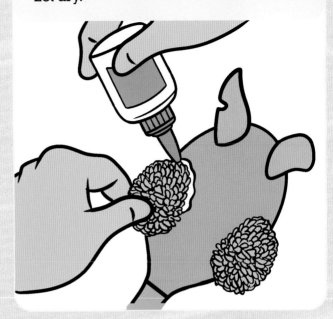

5

Glue buttons onto the front of the wooden spoon for the pup's eyes and nose. Let dry. Add any details with black marker.

DON'T LOSE IT, REUSE IT!

WAGGING CRAFT STICK PUPPETS

The pups are more than just a rescue team, they're friends. And the only way for friends to stay together is to play together! So make these craft sticks and you can show the PAW Patrol both on and off duty.

WHAT YOU NEED

- two craft sticks
- paint
- paintbrush
- black marker
- colored cardstock
- safety scissors
- glue

WHAT TO DO

1 Paint the craft sticks the same color as the pups. Let dry.

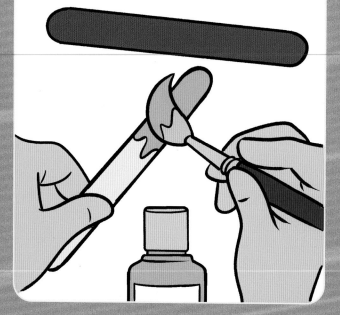

2 Add face details with black marker.

Cut out the pups' ears from colored cardstock, and glue them at the top of the craft sticks. Let dry.

A PAWFECT TEAM!

HOW TO PUT ON A PAWSOME PUPPET SHOW!

Here's how to make a pup-tastic theater to stage your show. All you'll need is: some paint, safety scissors, and a large cardboard box!

WHAT TO DO

1   Have the box opening at the back, and cut a big square hole at the front for the audience to watch the show through. Paint the box a light color inside, and a dark color outside. You could even add a strip of red material or tissue paper to each side of the square hole, like theater curtains!

2

Invite all your friends and family to the Opening Night of your show! Don't forget to tell them the date, time, and place of the performance, so they won't miss a moment.

3

Think about props. Will your puppets need to use anything as part of the show? A tool, a drink, or a vehicle? Try to find things from around the house to help, or you could make them from craft materials.

THE BEST IN SHOW ARE SURE TO PUT ON THE BEST SHOW!

FAN FAVORITES

Audiences love having snacks when they watch a show! Have some mouthwatering munchies and delicious drinks ready to serve your fans.

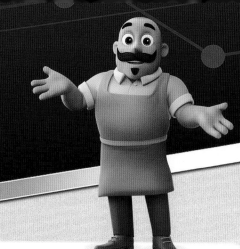

PUP-CORN

This crunchy, cheesy popcorn is PAWfect for munching on during the performance.

Ingredients:
- Plain popped, popcorn
- Melted butter
- Parmesan and/or cheddar cheese

Steps:
- Preheat the oven to 350 degrees F.
- Spread the popcorn out on a cookie sheet.
- Drip some butter over the top, followed by sprinkles of cheese.
- Pop into the oven for 5 minutes, or until the cheese starts bubbling.
- Leave to cool before pouring into bowls.

MR. PORTER'S PUNCH

Slurp! This delicious fruity drink will keep your audience cool in a hot theater.

Ingredients:
- 3 cups orange juice
- 3 cups pineapple juice
- 3 cups mango juice
- Ice cubes
- Sliced oranges for garnish (optional)
- Curly straws

Steps:
- Mix the fruit juices together in a pitcher.
- Put a few ice cubes in each glass, then pour over the fruit juice mix.
- Add an orange slice and curly straw to each glass.

Bone Biscuits

They might be shaped like dog biscuits, but these tasty treats are just for humans!

Ingredients:
- 7/8 cup unsalted butter, softened
- 1 1/4 cups superfine sugar
- 1/4 tsp vanilla extract
- 1 egg
- 3 1/5 cups plain/all-purpose flour
- A pinch of salt
- 1/2 tsp cream of tartar

Steps:
- Preheat the oven to 325 degrees F.
- Mix the butter, sugar, and vanilla extract, then stir in the egg.
- Add the flour, salt, and cream of tartar, then knead together.
- On a flour-covered surface, roll out the dough until it's about ½-inch thick.
- Use cutters to make bone-shaped biscuits, then place them on cookie sheets.
- Pop into the oven for 10 minutes, or until they turn golden.
- Leave to cool before placing on a serving plate.